A CLEAN EARTH
THE GEOTHERMAL STORY

Robyn C. Friend
and
Judith Love Cohen

ILLUSTRATIONS:
David A. Katz

Editing:
Lee Rathbone

Cascade
Pass, Inc.
www.CascadePass.com

Copyright © 2010 by Cascade Pass, Inc.
Published by Cascade Pass, Inc.
4223 Glencoe Avenue, Suite C-105
Marina del Rey, CA 90292-8801
Phone: (310) 305-0210
Web Site: http://www.CascadePass.com
Printed in China by South China Printing Co. Ltd

A Clean Earth: The Geothermal Story was written by Robyn C. Friend and Judith Love Cohen, and edited by Lee Rathbone designed and illustrated by David Katz.

This book is one of a series that emphasizes the environment and the value of preserving it by depicting what real people are doing to meet the challenges.

Other books in the series include:
A Clean Planet: The Solar Power Story
A Clean City: The Green Construction Story
A Clean Sky: The Global Warming Story
A Clean Sea: The Rachel Carson Story

Library of Congress Cataloging-in-Publication Data

Friend, Robyn C., 1955-
      A clean earth : the geothermal story / Robyn C. Friend and Judith Love Cohen ; edited by Lee Rathbone. – 1st ed.
          p. cm.
Includes bibliographical references and index.
          ISBN 1-880599-98-8 (pbk.) – ISBN 1-880599-99-6 (hard cover)
          1. Environmental management. 2. Environmental protection. 3. Global warming. 4. Environmentalism. I. Cohen, Judith Love, 1933- II. Rathbone, Lee. III. Title.
TD170.2.F72 2010
333.8'8–dc22   2010039190

Introduction

When we think about energy to power our lives, we look out the window and see the sun and we are aware that it is the most important source of energy for all life on our planet Earth. Its huge supply of energy keeps us warm, grows our food and lights our day. But what we don't see, and what many of us don't know, is that underneath our feet, deep inside the Earth, is enough energy to supply the energy needs of mankind for thousands of years!

This book tells the story of *geothermal* power, what it is, what it can do, and how we can find and use this energy to help us have a cleaner Earth.

This is the fifth book in Cascade Pass's environmental series dedicated to our planet Earth's resources – the oceans, the skies, the rainforests, the deserts, the hot springs … all those special environments that are shared by varieties of animals and plants – and to those whose efforts have protected them. *A Clean Earth: The Geothermal Story* explains the power of our Earth's interior, the heat energy provided by nature, and how we can use its warmth and power without polluting our environment.

When you walk outside, or hike in the mountains, or when you carefully walk into the ocean at the beach, you experience the ground under your feet as a hard, cold surface. It isn't burning like the surface of the sun. But, inside, at the Earth's *core*, 4,000 miles down, the temperature is extremely hot, over 9,000 degrees Fahrenheit! That would melt anything including steel, or even rock.

This heat is called *geothermal* heat, *geo* from the Greek word for Earth and *therme* from the Greek word for heat.

The extreme heat from the Earth's core flows outward to the Earth's *mantle* where the temperature remains very high (still between 1,000 and 1,500 degrees Fahrenheit at the bottom of the Earth's *crust*) and is certainly hot enough to melt the surrounding rock. The hot liquid rock is called *magma*. The magma moves up through the Earth's crust, carrying the heat from below.

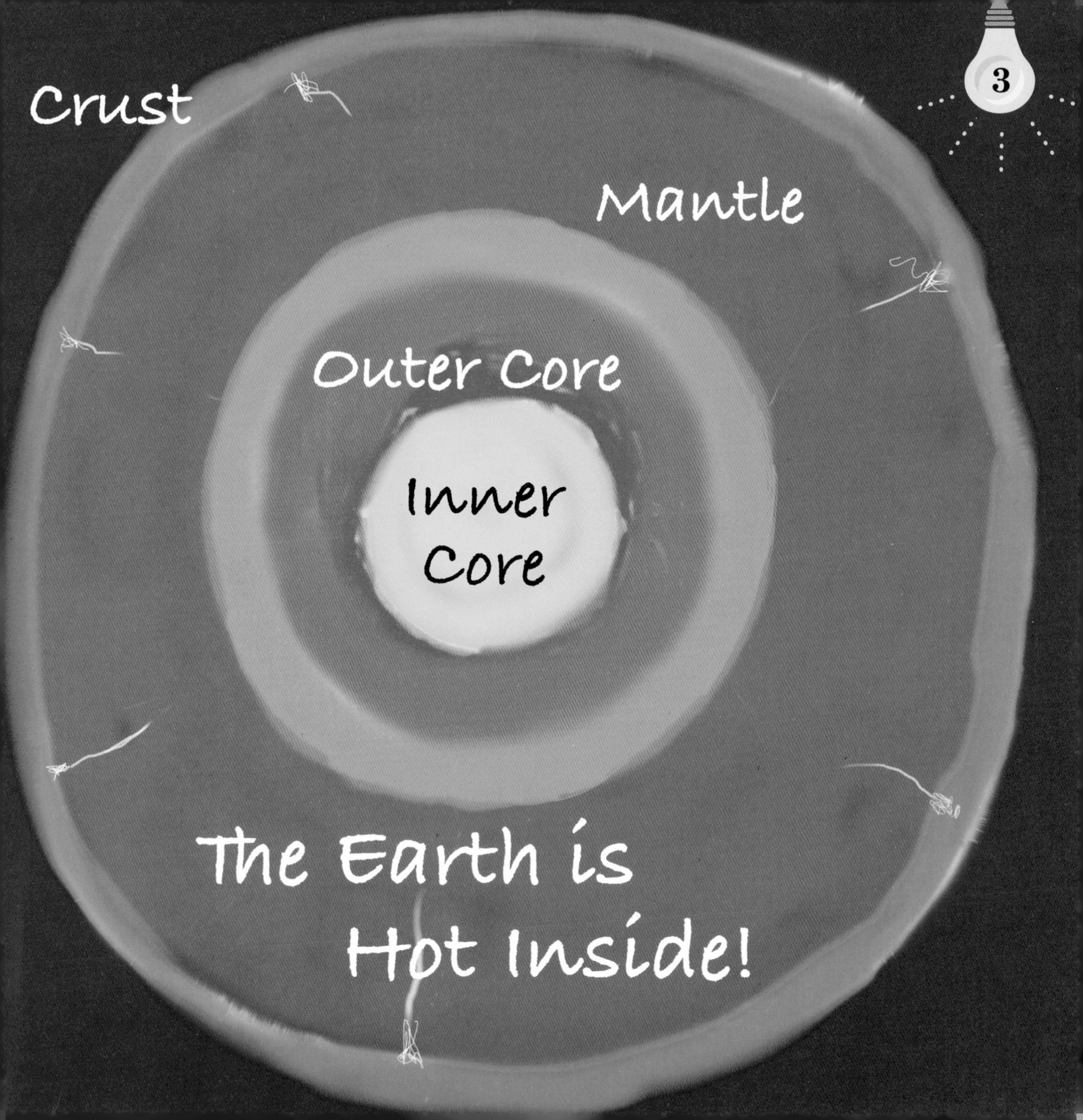
Crust
Mantle
Outer Core
Inner Core
The Earth is Hot Inside!

All of this is happening and we never see it! How do we know what is going on beneath the Earth's surface? Well, have you ever seen a *volcano*? Have you seen pictures or movies where a powerful volcano erupts? What causes it to happen?

There are places on the surface of the Earth where there are cracks or *fault* lines. The magma can find its way up through a crack and spill out onto the Earth's surface and we call it *lava*. Sometimes it builds up a small cone or large mountain called a *volcano*.

If there isn't a volcano around to tell us where there is underground heat energy, how can we find it? Sometimes rainwater seeps deep into the Earth through these cracks, and the magma heats the water. Some of this hot geothermal water travels back up through the cracks and reaches the surface as *geysers* or *hot springs*.

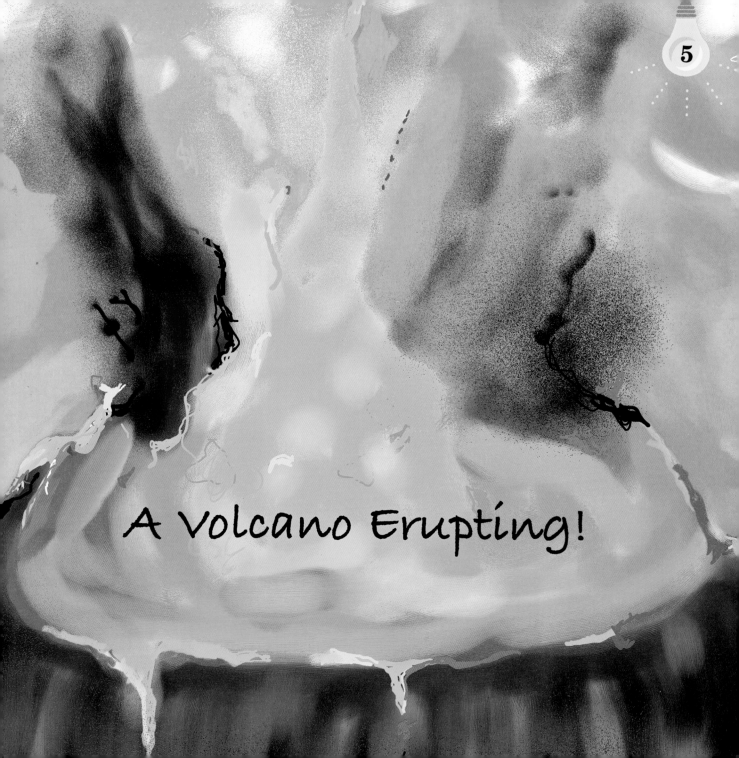

A Volcano Erupting!

But where are these cracks? What causes them?

The crust of the Earth is not a solid piece, but since it is rather cool, hard and brittle, it is broken up into many pieces, called *tectonic plates*. These plates move around very slowly and bump into each other, or ride-up over the top of one another. They crack, bend, and wrinkle up where they bump together, and that causes *earthquakes*. The earthquakes may be scary, but they serve an important function here. The cracks in the Earth that are created when the plates move are the way the geothermal energy can reach the surface of the Earth and form geysers and hot springs. The places that have earthquake faults, like Southern California, Japan, and Indonesia, are also the places where there is a lot of geothermal energy near the surface. And of course the places that don't have these faults, like Florida or New York or Great Britain, don't have the geothermal energy.

A Geyser:
The Geothermal Energy is Here!

People have been using geothermal energy directly for centuries. Thousands of years ago, the Romans and the Native Americans learned to use the geothermal water that flowed from the Earth's surface as hot springs. They relaxed in community baths or used the hot springs water for cooking, heating their homes and as medicine to treat eye and skin diseases.

Of course we can also relax in hot springs, and use the hot water in greenhouses and fish farms. And district heating systems in many areas use the hot water to heat houses, sidewalks, and soil.

But now we don't have to wait for the hot water to come up to the surface. We can drill wells right down into the deep underground geothermal *reservoirs* to bring the hot water up. Then once the hot water and steam travel to the surface, we can generate electricity in power plants.

Okay, we drill a well, and reach the geothermal reservoir. How do we actually generate the wonderful thing called electricity? What process is used?

Well, that depends on what actually is in the particular geothermal reservoir: there can be steam or hot water or both. And the temperature of the water can be super high (700 degrees Fahrenheit instead of the 210 degrees that boils water on your stove) or it can be less than 300 degrees. There are different processes that deal with the different types of water and steam found in these reservoirs.

One common process that is used when the water is superheated is a "flash" steam power plant. A *production well* brings the superheated water up to the surface. Some of the water boils to high pressure steam and turns the *turbine* blades of the generator to make electricity. The remaining hot water and the used steam that cools into water are pumped back into the reservoir through an *injection well*.

Flash Steam Plant

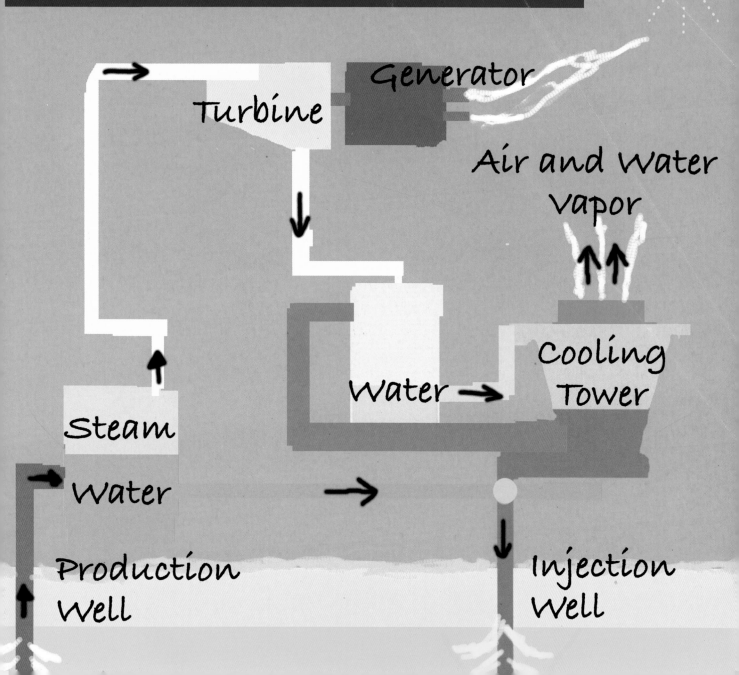

Wait a minute, we had hot water; how did it become steam? When we heat water in a tea kettle, we can hear the water become steam as the tea kettle whistles. But if it is just water, how does it become steam?

Have you ever taken a closed can of soda and shaken it? What happens when you open it? The liquid sprays all over! Shaking the can causes an increase in pressure in the liquid, so that when it is released by opening the top, the liquid expands into spray.

Superheated water becomes steam in a similar way. Magma close to the bottom of the reservoir and the high pressure in the reservoir causes the water to be superheated in the first place. When the superheated water reaches the top of the well, the pressure is released and the water expands into spray or steam!

Water
Becoming
Steam!

Now we know how geothermal power works. How do we find where the geothermal energy is? We asked Terra-Gen, one of the largest geothermal energy companies in the United States. They said that near geysers, hot springs and volcanoes there are regions where rocks have been changed a bit by the heat and hot water. Their geoscientists recognize these clues and study these areas very closely. This is where you find "hot spots" where magma has moved close to the surface, perhaps following a deep fracture, and where water has seeped down deep and collected in a large underground geothermal reservoir. Once you know what to look for, you are well on your way.

In today's world, there are many tools to help. For instance, satellites can do *infra-red scans* while flying above likely areas. What is infra-red? Light comes in three forms: First, there is visible light, for example the sunshine and the colors of the rainbow. Second, there is the ultra-violet light, that is the part of sunshine that we can't see but gives us sunburn. The third form is infra-red light. Infra-red light rays are given off by heat, and the infra-red scanning instruments make measurements that can be used to create infra-red maps which show these "hot spots."

Geologists can then study the rocks in "hot spot" areas and identify places for further exploration.

Studying
an Infra-Red
Map!

Terra-Gen's focus is not only in finding geothermal resources, but in developing them and using them to create electricity.

When a hot spot is located in a promising area, a small hole will be drilled with a truck-mounted rig to determine the temperature of the water and the type of rocks. If the temperature gets hotter very quickly as it goes down the hole, scientists make an estimate of the size and location of the geothermal resource, and analyze what it consists of: dry steam, steam and hot water, or mostly hot water.

Now a much larger and deeper well will be drilled. Drilling a geothermal well is very similar to drilling an oil well. A huge drill rig is required to drill a production well. It may drill down more than two miles looking for the geothermal reservoir. Drilling will go on 24 hours a day. If there is a good geothermal reservoir at the bottom, the drill rig is removed and a *well head* with control equipment is bolted on top of the well. Think of a faucet turning the water on or off in your bathtub. The control equipment is like a faucet for the hot water in the geothermal reservoir.

Drilling a Well!

Remember that steam from the production well powers the turbine blades of the generator. This generates electricity. When the steam cools, it turns back into water which is pumped back down into the reservoir through an injection well.

Typical electric generators use steam to spin the turbine blades, but in this case no fossil fuel is burned, and no smoke is generated, so there are no emissions except for steam.

At Coso Hot Springs, in China Lake, California, in addition to generating the electricity to supply power to the Naval Air Station, electricity can be generated for an estimated 250,000 California homes!

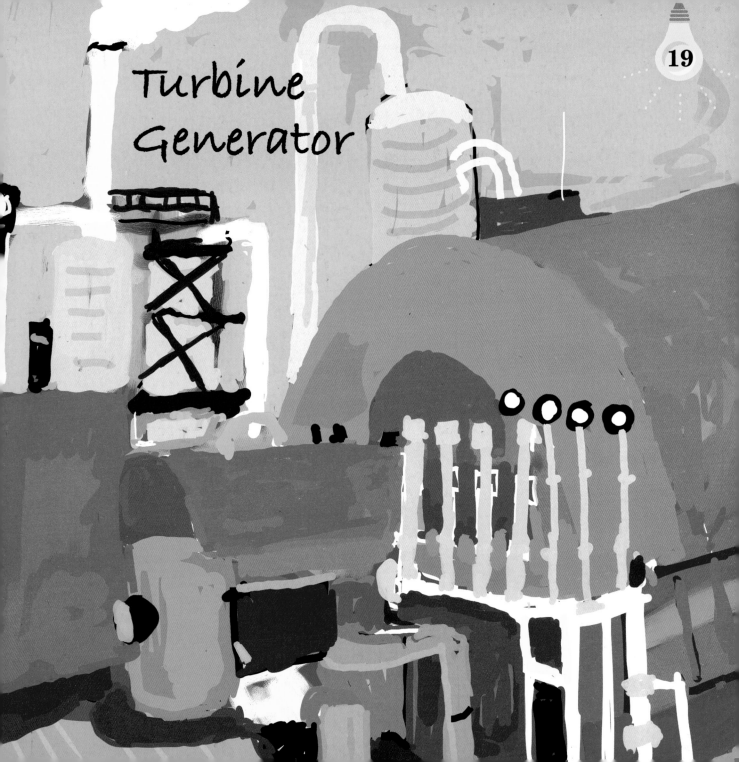

Turbine
Generator

19

Southern California Edison is a power company that buys electricity from geothermal energy companies like Terra-Gen and arranges to deliver it to their customers. Today, about 10% of all the electricity Southern California Edison delivers to its 5 million customers is created with geothermal energy!

Since the geothermal electrical energy is generated at the geothermal reservoir, the power must be collected and transmitted down a wire by those tall steel towers with long drooping wires to the *electrical grid*.

Since geothermal resources are often located far from urban areas, the transmission is an important part of the process. In California, the California Independent System Operator (CA-ISO) transmits electricity it receives from generator sites, through the electrical grid, to distributors, and on to homes and businesses.

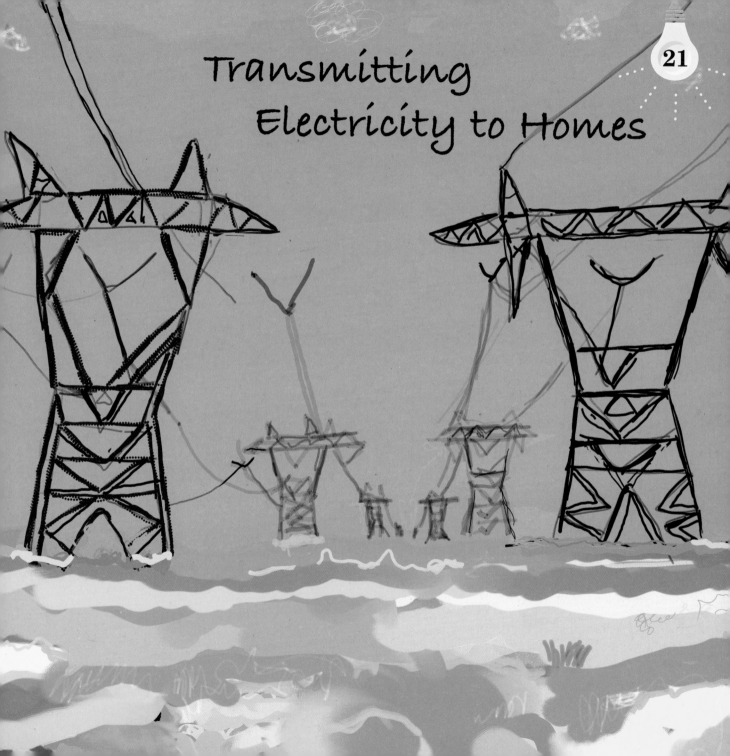

Transmitting Electricity to Homes

How does using geothermal energy help our Planet Earth stay cleaner?

Clean Energy. Geothermal power plants, like wind and solar power plants, do not have to burn fossil fuels or natural gas to generate steam to turn the turbines. This helps to conserve fossil fuels, which are not renewable, and by decreasing the use of these fuels, we reduce the emissions that harm our atmosphere. There is no smoky air around geothermal power plants, which is good for forests, farm crops, farm animals, local wildlife, and people.

Easy on the Land. The land area required for geothermal power plants is smaller for each megawatt of electrical energy than for almost every other type of power plant. Geothermal sites do not require damming of rivers, and there are no mine shafts, waste heaps, or oil spills.

Reliable. Geothermal power plants are designed to run 24 hours a day, every day. They sit right on top of their fuel sources; therefore, weather or natural disasters don't interrupt the supply of fuel.

A Clean Clear Sky!

Flexible. Geothermal power plants can be designed to be in small units, so they can start small and have more units added when more electricity is needed.

Economical. Money does not have to be spent to import fuel. Geothermal energy is right there where the power plant is and can be distributed to nearby areas.

Helps developing countries grow. Geothermal projects can offer all the benefits already listed to help developing countries grow without pollution. Installation in remote locations, far from the "electrical grid" can raise the standard of living and quality of life.

Power Plant
at COSO Hot Springs!

As we have seen, the geothermal reservoirs that are close enough to the surface to be used are in areas where the Earth's crust has fractured as the plates bump into each other, bend, and crack. These are mostly around the Pacific Ocean: the mountains of South America, Central America, Mexico, the Cascade mountains of the United States and Canada, the Aleutian Islands of Alaska, the Kamchatka Peninsula of Russia, Japan, the Philippines, Indonesia and New Zealand.

It is therefore not surprising that among the largest producers of geothermal energy are the United States, Japan, Indonesia, the Philippines and New Zealand. There are several other geothermal hot spots in Iceland and Italy that are used to generate power.

What are some ways to use geothermal energy without making it into electricity?

Geothermally heated water is used around the world, and when we use it instead of heating water, we save energy!

We use it to soak in hot springs and health spas.

We use it to help grow flowers and vegetables in greenhouses even when it's snowing outside.

We use it to help fish, shrimp, abalone, and alligators grow faster.

We use it in industry to pasteurize milk, to dry onions and lumber and to wash wool.

And it can be used to heat buildings by running hot water where the heat is transferred to the building's heating system.

COSO Hot Springs

You Can Help!

The best thing you can do to help generate clean power through geothermal energy is to become a scientist or engineer, so that you can help locate geothermal reservoirs, find ways to generate electrical power more efficiently, find better ways to use the energy generated and help to make it easier for geothermal power to be used throughout the world.

Careers in Geothermal Energy

Geophysicist: Geophysics is the study of the whole Earth, by scientific observation of its physical properties. As a geophysicist you would use geophysical data to learn about the movement of tectonic plates, and help to find underground geothermal reservoirs.

Geochemist: Geochemistry is the study of the chemical composition of the Earth, and the chemical processes and reactions of rocks, water, and soils. As a geochemist, you could discover new ways to locate underground geothermal reservoirs by looking at rocks found near geothermal "hot spots."

Geologist: Geology is the study of the material that constitutes the Earth, and of the Earth as a whole. It includes the study of the composition, structure, physical properties, dynamics, and history of Earth materials, and the processes by which they are formed, moved, and changed. As a geologist, you could discover new places to drill for geothermal steam and hot water.

Seismologist: Seismology is the study of earthquakes. As a seismologist, you would study the movements of tectonic plates, and ways to find underground geothermal reservoirs.

Well Driller: As a well driller, you would work on the equipment that drills down through the Earth's crust to look for geothermal reservoirs, and on production and injection wells.

Electrical Engineer: As an electrical engineer, you could find more efficient ways to transfer the power of geothermal energy into electricity for public use.

Mechanical Engineer: As a mechanical engineer, you could design and build new power generation plants that use the hot water in geothermal reservoirs more efficiently.

Power Plant Construction Worker: As a power plant construction worker, you would help build the power generation facility that converts steam and hot water from the geothermal reservoir into electricity and transmits it to the electrical grid.

Power Plant Operator: As a power plant operator, you would help to run the equipment that brings the steam and hot water out of the geothermal reservoir, delivers it to the power generation facility that converts the geothermal energy into electricity and transmits it to the electrical grid.

Now you know where geothermal energy comes from and how it is used to create electrical power. And you know what different scientists and other professionals do to make it all happen. If you work hard in school and study the sciences, you can help turn geothermal energy into cheap and clean electricity, too!

FUN FACTS

Did you know that California has more geothermal resources than anywhere else in the world?

In 1847 a huge dry steam geothermal source was discovered in Northern California. It was first used for a hot springs resort, then later was used to generate electrical power.

The first geothermal power plant in the U.S. was built at The Geysers in Northern California, in 1962. It is still in operation today, and is the largest geothermal power plant in the world!

The Romans used the water from hot springs to heat their baths 2000 years ago!

The first use of geothermal steam to produce electric power was in the Lardarello region of Italy in 1904; we get geothermal power from the same geothermal fields today. During the Middle Ages wars were fought in Lardarello over the rights to use these geothermally-heated waters.

The first major liquid-dominated geothermal power plant was built in New Zealand in 1958.

The tectonic plates that create cracks in the Earth's surface at their edges move at about the same rate as your fingernails grow.

Geothermal drilling can go down as much as 2 miles deep, and more.

Did you know that geothermal power plants have been built in the middle of crop lands, recreational forests, deserts, and tropical forests?

And the power plants have no negative effect on the surrounding environment.

Geothermal power plants all over the world provide 8,200 megawatts of power to 60 million people, mostly in developing countries.

To find out more fun facts, visit:

http://geothermal.marin.org/GEOpresentation/sld004.htm

http://geothermal.marin.org/pwrheat.html

http://www.sce.com/PowerandEnvironment/Renewables/Geothermal.htm

GLOSSARY

Core: The center of the Earth where it is so hot that rock melts.

Crust: A crust is the hard outer layer of something, like the crust on bread. The crust of the Earth is the outermost solid shell of hard rock, about 22 miles thick.

Earthquake: An earthquake occurs when some part of the Earth's crust shifts suddenly, causing everything on the surface to shake.

Electrical grid: A network of wires that distributes electrical power throughout an area, such as the continental United States.

Fault: A crack in the surface of the Earth, usually caused by an earthquake.

Geothermal: This is a word that is formed by two Greek words that together mean "heat from the Earth: "geo" from the Greek word for Earth and "therme" from the Greek word for heat.

Geyser: When rainwater seeps into the Earth's crust and gets heated by the magma (hot liquid rock) it goes up through a crack or fault in the crust and explodes into a jet of hot water and steam, called a geyser, pronounced "guy-zer."

Hot spring: A hot spring is the place where water heated by magma (hot liquid rock) under the Earth's crust comes to the surface and forms pools of very hot water.

Infra-red scans: Infra-red light waves are longer than visible light waves, and are therefore not visible to the unaided human eye. Special sensors, called IR (infra-red) sensors on satellites can check for underground heat by looking for areas on the surface of the Earth that radiate in the infra-red part of the light spectrum.

Injection well: An injection well takes cooled water from the surface where it was used to turn a turbine to generate electricity and pipes it back into the reservoir, to be reheated by the Earth's core heat.

Lava: Hot liquid rock that comes up through the Earth's surface.

Magma: Rock that is so hot it is liquid.

Magma Chamber: A large underground pool of magma, under great pressure. The pressure can cause fractures in the surrounding rock, allowing magma to escape to the surface in a volcanic eruption.

Mantle: The Earth's mantle is a nearly 2,000 mile thick layer of mostly solid rock between the hot liquid core of the Earth and its hard outer crust. The mantle is about 90 per cent of the Earth's entire volume.

Production well: A production well brings the steam and hot water up from the reservoir to the surface where it can be used to generate power.

Reservoir: A reservoir is a large container for holding something, usually liquid, and often water. Reservoirs can be man-made (like a big water tank), or natural, like a lake, or a place deep underground where water seeps under the surface and collects.

Tectonic plates: The huge landmasses that rise out of the oceans and form the continents are actually islands of solid rock floating above magma. These islands can move around (very slowly!) and sometimes bump into each other. The Himalayas Mountains were formed by the tectonic plate of India bumping into the tectonic plate of Asia.

Turbine: A rotary engine that takes energy from a fluid flow, like water or steam, and converts it into useful work.

Volcano: A place on the surface of the Earth where hot liquid rock comes up to the surface. The rock cools to hardness and eventually after many eruptions of lava a cone of rock is formed on the Earth's surface.

Well head: A well head is equipment at the surface of a well that makes it possible to control the flow of fluid (gas, oil, or water), and provides a seal to prevent leaks.

A CLEAN PLANET: THE GEOTHERMAL STORY

LESSON PLAN 1

PURPOSE: To understand what volcanoes look like.

MATERIALS: Scissors, glue, shoe boxes, art supplies (paper, crayons, paints, colored pencils and clay).

PROCEDURES: Have children take the shoe box and create an area that will contain a volcano. surrounded by other mountains, lakes, rivers, etc. They should create an eruption with hot molten lava running down the side of the volcano.

CONCLUSIONS: What is coming out of the volcano?
Where did it come from?
How did it get past the Earth's crust?

RESOURCES: Pictures of erupting volcanoes from the internet.

LESSON PLAN 2

PURPOSE: To understand what the inside of the Earth is like: hot!

MATERIALS: Art supplies (paper, crayons, paints, colored pencils and glitter).

PROCEDURE: Have children make a large circle to represent the Earth cut open. Now have them describe and then draw the layers inside the Earth: a solid and very hot inner core, a liquid outer core, a semi-melted mantle, and finally a solid crust that we like and walk on.

CONCLUSIONS: Heat flows outward from the inside of the Earth. The crust separates us from the hot inside.

LESSON PLAN 3

PURPOSE: To understand where geothermal resources are found and how they can be located.

MATERIALS: Copies of world maps, or globes, art supplies (paper, pencils, crayons, marker pens, and/or gold stars or similar stick-on colors).

PROCEDURE: Have children look at the world map or atlas and locate their home area with oceans, lakes, and mountains nearby. Then have children look at resources such as travel books around the world. Have them make a list of volcanoes and geysers. For example: The Geysers in Sonoma County, California or Mount Rainier, near Seattle Washington. After they have created a list, they should locate the areas on their map or globe and mark them with stars, crayon, or marker pen. After they have marked a number of these areas, does there seem to be a pattern or connection between them?

CONCLUSIONS: Where are these volcanic and geyser areas located?
What is the connection?
What is there about the areas that make them home to such things?

RESOURCES: Books about volcanoes and geysers, or geothermal books such as *"Geothermal Energy as a Source of Electricity: A Worldwide Survey"* by Ronald DiPippo.

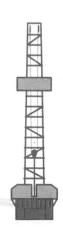

ABOUT THE CONTRIBUTORS:

DAN CHASE, **contributor**, is a Contract Negotiator with Southern California Edison's Renewable & Alternative Power Department. He has over 32 years experience in the energy industry including project development, analysis, finance, and operations. He has worked intermittently in the geothermal industry since 1978 on projects in Mexico, Indonesia, Hawaii, Nevada, and California.

JOSEPH GRECO, **Senior Vice President**, Terra-Gen Power, LLC (Reno, NV). Responsible for asset management and expansion of Terra-Gen's geothermal and solar portfolio as well as Terra-Gen's governmental affairs efforts. Joined the Terra-Gen team following acquisition of the Caithness Energy renewable portfolio in December of 2007. While at Caithness held the position of Vice President – Western Region with responsibility for the geothermal and solar portfolio as well natural gas facility development. Prior to joining Caithness in January 2001, served for 6 years at UAE Energy Operation's Corp., an Independent Energy Producer focused on fossil and biomass power generation technologies. Responsibilities for UAE included asset management, operations and maintenance management, concluding as Vice President of Development for the West Coast. Prior to joining UAE, held various management positions at Consolidated Edison of New York. 1987 graduate of Manhattan College, with Bachelors of Science in Mechanical Engineering.

ELLEN ALLMAN, **Senior Business Manager**, Terra-Gen Power, LLC (Reno, NV). Responsible for management of Nevada assets and support of expansion of Terra-Gen's West Coast geothermal portfolio. President of the Nevada Geothermal Council. Prior to joining Terra-Gen in May 2001, provided long term planning for 18 months at Kaiser Aluminum in Spokane, Washington. Prior to Kaiser, served 8 years in various locations and positions with ARCO Oil & Gas Company, concluding as a Planning & Evaluation Specialist. Prior to joining ARCO, performed engineering at Long Island Lighting Co. of New York. 1992 Masters graduate of Yale School of Management, 1985 graduate of Cooper Union School of Engineering with Bachelors of Chemical Engineering.

ABOUT THE AUTHORS:

ROBYN C. FRIEND, **author**, is a singer, dancer, choreographer, and writer. She earned a Ph.D. in Iranian Linguistics at UCLA, and promptly launched a twenty-year career building spacecraft. She has written for both scholarly and popular publications on a wide variety of subjects, including folkloric dance, world music, linguistics, travel, and the exploration of Mars by balloon.

JUDITH LOVE COHEN, **author**, is a Registered Professional Electrical Engineer with bachelor's and master's degrees in engineering from the University of Southern California and University of California, Los Angeles. She has written plays, screenplays, and newspaper articles in addition to her series of children's books that began with *You Can Be a Woman Engineer*.

ABOUT THE ILLUSTRATOR:

DAVID ARTHUR KATZ, **illustrator**, received his training in art education and holds a master's degree from the University of South Florida. He is a credentialed teacher in the Los Angeles Unified School District. His involvement in the arts has encompassed animation, illustration, and playwriting, poetry, and songwriting. His drawings and animations are presently being collected in museums.

Graphic materials created by KANA TATEKAWA, Momo Communications, Inc.

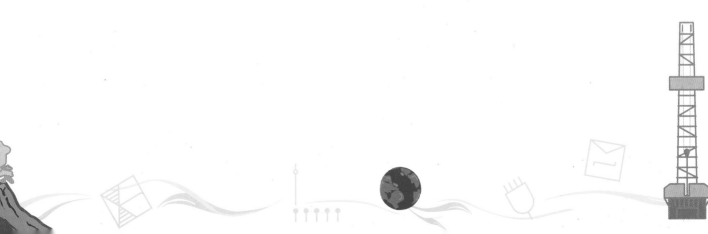

For more than a century, **Southern California Edison** has remained committed to environmental protection. We are proud of our leadership on many key initiatives that will help preserve and enhance our communities and our world for future generations.

SOUTHERN CALIFORNIA
EDISON

An *EDISON INTERNATIONAL* Company

Terra-Gen Power is a renewable energy company focused on geothermal, wind and solar generation. Terra-Gen Power owns 331 megawatts (MW), net equity, in 21 operating renewable energy projects across the Western United

C L E A N   E N E R G Y

States. Wholly owned subsidiaries, Terra-Gen Operating Company and Coso Operating Company, operate and manage most of the projects. The company primarily sells the output of the renewable energy projects to load serving entities under long-term

C L E A N   E A R T H

power purchase agreements. Terra-Gen Power is developing up to 5,000 MWs of new wind, solar and geothermal projects. For more information please visit Terra-Gen Power's website.

www.terra-genpower.com

Terra-Gen Power, LLC